Your Get Up and Go 2017

Your diary conta

Messages
of hope and encourage

Wisdom
from yesterday for today and tomorrow

Thoughts
of gratitude and appreciation

Words
of peace and love

Inspiration
for when you want it

Humour
to laugh at the funny side of life

Space
for your personal goals and dreams

Optimism
to live life with a positive view

Motivation
for when you need it

*There comes a day
when you realise that turning the page
is the best feeling in the world,
for you realise
there is more to the book
than the page you are stuck on.*

2017 BANK AND PUBLIC HOLIDAYS

REPUBLIC OF IRELAND
New Year's Day, 1 January;
St Patrick's Day, 17 March;
Good Friday, 14 April;
Easter Monday, 17 April;
May Day, 1 May;
June Holiday, 5 June;
August Holiday, 7 August;
October Holiday, 30 October;
Christmas Day, 25 December;
St Stephen's Day, 26 December.

NORTHERN IRELAND
New Year's Day, 1 January;
Good Friday, 14 April;
May Day Holiday, 1 May;
Orangemen's Holiday, 12 July;
Christmas Day, 25 December;
St Patrick's Day, 17 March;
Easter Monday, 17 April;
Spring Bank Holiday, 29 May;
Summer Bank Holiday, 28 August;
Boxing Day, 26 December.

ENGLAND, SCOTLAND AND WALES
New Year's Day, 1 January;
Easter Monday, 17 Aprilh;
Spring Bank Holiday, 29 May;
Christmas Day, 25 December;
Good Friday, 14 April;
May Day Holiday, 1 May;
Summer Bank Holiday, 28 August;
Boxing Day, 26 December.

UNITED STATES OF AMERICA
New Year's Day, 1 January;
Presidents' Day, 20 February;
Independence Day, 4 July;
Columbus Day, 9 October;
Thanksgiving Day, 23 November;
Martin Luther King Day, 16 January;
Memorial Day, 29 May;
Labour Day, 4 September;
Veterans Day, 11 November;
Christmas Day, 25 December.

CANADA
New Year's Day, 1 January;
Heritage Day, 20 February;
St Patrick's Day, 17 March;
Easter Monday, 17 April;
Canada Day, 1 July;
Thanksgiving Day, 9 October;
Christmas Day, 25 December;
Family Day, 20 February;
Commonwealth Day, 13 March;
Good Friday, 14 April;
Victoria Day 22 May;
Labour Day, 4 Sept;
Rememberance Day, 11 November;
Boxing Day, 26 December.

AUSTRALIA (NATIONAL HOLIDAYS)
New Year's Day, 1 January;
Good Friday, 14 April;
Anzac Day 25 April;
Christmas Day, 25 December;
Australia Day, 26 January;
Easter Monday, 17 April;
Queen's Birthday, 25 September;
Boxing Day, 26 December.

2017 CALENDAR

January 2017

No.	Su	Mo	Tu	We	Th	Fr	Sa
1	1	2	3	4	5	6	7
2	8	9	10	11	12	13	14
3	15	16	17	18	19	20	21
4	22	23	24	25	26	27	28
5	29	30	31				

February 2017

No.	Su	Mo	Tu	We	Th	Fr	Sa
5				1	2	3	4
6	5	6	7	8	9	10	11
7	12	13	14	15	16	17	18
8	19	20	21	22	23	24	25
9	26	27	28				

March 2017

No.	Su	Mo	Tu	We	Th	Fr	Sa
9				1	2	3	4
10	5	6	7	8	9	10	11
11	12	13	14	15	16	17	18
12	19	20	21	22	23	24	25
13	26	27	28	29	30	31	

April 2017

No.	Su	Mo	Tu	We	Th	Fr	Sa
13							1
14	2	3	4	5	6	7	8
15	9	10	11	12	13	14	15
16	16	17	18	19	20	21	22
17	23	24	25	26	27	28	29
18	30						

May 2017

No.	Su	Mo	Tu	We	Th	Fr	Sa
18		1	2	3	4	5	6
19	7	8	9	10	11	12	13
20	14	15	16	17	18	19	20
21	21	22	23	24	25	26	27
22	28	29	30	31			

June 2017

No.	Su	Mo	Tu	We	Th	Fr	Sa
22					1	2	3
23	4	5	6	7	8	9	10
24	11	12	13	14	15	16	17
25	18	19	20	21	22	23	24
26	25	26	27	28	29	30	

July 2017

No.	Su	Mo	Tu	We	Th	Fr	Sa
26							1
27	2	3	4	5	6	7	8
28	9	10	11	12	13	14	15
29	16	17	18	19	20	21	22
30	23	24	25	26	27	28	29
31	30	31					

August 2017

No.	Su	Mo	Tu	We	Th	Fr	Sa
31			1	2	3	4	5
32	6	7	8	9	10	11	12
33	13	14	15	16	17	18	19
34	20	21	22	23	24	25	26
35	27	28	29	30	31		

September 2017

No.	Su	Mo	Tu	We	Th	Fr	Sa
35						1	2
36	3	4	5	6	7	8	9
37	10	11	12	13	14	15	16
38	17	18	19	20	21	22	23
39	24	25	26	27	28	29	30

October 2017

No.	Su	Mo	Tu	We	Th	Fr	Sa
40	1	2	3	4	5	6	7
41	8	9	10	11	12	13	14
42	15	16	17	18	19	20	21
43	22	23	24	25	26	27	28
44	29	30	31				

November 2017

No.	Su	Mo	Tu	We	Th	Fr	Sa
44				1	2	3	4
45	5	6	7	8	9	10	11
46	12	13	14	15	16	17	18
47	19	20	21	22	23	24	25
48	26	27	28	29	30		

December 2017

No.	Su	Mo	Tu	We	Th	Fr	Sa
48						1	2
49	3	4	5	6	7	8	9
50	10	11	12	13	14	15	16
51	17	18	19	20	21	22	23
52	24	25	26	27	28	29	30
1	31						

Forgive the past – let it go
Live the present – the power of now
Create the future – thoughts become things

The finest gift you can give anyone is the gift of encouragement. Yet, almost no one gets the encouragement they need to grow to their full potential. If everyone received the encouragement they need to grow, the genius in everyone would blossom and the world would produce abundance beyond our wildest dreams.

This diary belongs to: _____

Address: _____

Telephone: _____

Email: _____

EMERGENCY TELEPHONE NUMBERS

_____

_____

_____

Your diary contains 148 pages of inspiration!
Enjoy every page!

sprıocanna
GOALS
EANÁIR
JANUARY

_____
_____
_____
_____
_____
_____
_____
_____
_____
_____
_____
_____

The world will change for the better
when people decide they are
sick and tired of being sick and
tired of the way the world is, and
decide to change it themselves.

Más maith leat siocháin,
cairdeas agus moladh; éist,
feic agus fan balbh.

If you wish for peace,
friendship and praise;
listen, look and stay mute.

JANUARY

What the New Year brings to you will depend
a great deal on what you bring to the New Year.

Vern McLellan

A NEW YEAR

Another fresh new year is here ...
Another year to live!
To banish worry, doubt, and fear,
To love and laugh and give!
This bright new year is given me
To live each day with zest ...
To daily grow and try to be
My highest and my best!
I have the opportunity
Once more to right some wrongs,
To pray for peace, to plant a tree,
And sing more joyful songs!

William Arthur Ward

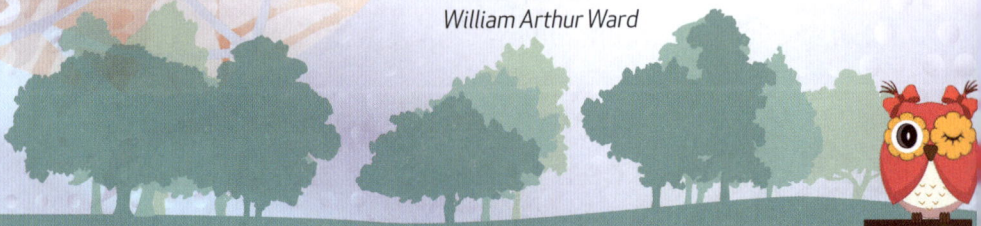

SUNDAY **1**
HAPPY NEW YEAR!

Get up and Go for 2017

Let the day unfold.
Expect the unexpected.
Surrender to miracles.
Never forget you are not alone.
See the goodness in others.
Be present.
Speak kindly.
Impart love.
Give thanks.

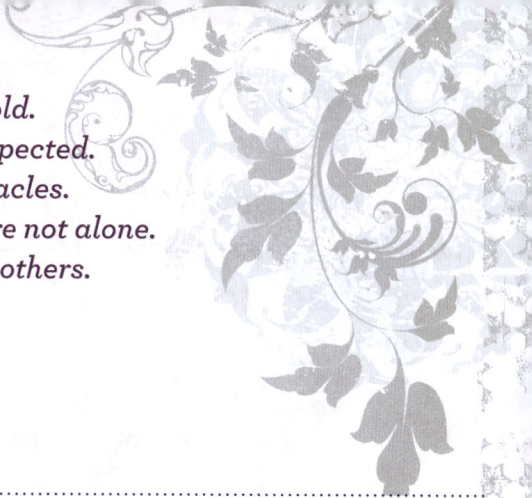

MONDAY **2**

Fill your mind with new positive thinking

TUESDAY **3**

Appreciate your home and your family

WEDNESDAY **4**

Each day is a new opportunity

THURSDAY **5**

You are in charge of the thoughts you think

JANUARY

*If we understood the power of our thoughts,
we would guard them more closely.
If we understood the awesome power of our words,
we would prefer silence to almost anything negative.
In our thoughts and words we create our own
weaknesses and our own strengths.
Our limitations and joys
begin in our hearts.
We can always replace
negative with positive.*

Betty Eadie

FRIDAY **6**

Time spent criticsising others is wasted time

SATURDAY **7**

Ask for guidance and it will always be available to you

SUNDAY **8**

Happiness attracts happiness

To love a person is to see all of their magic, and to remind them of it when they have forgotten.

You Raise Me Up

When I am down and, oh, my soul, so weary;
When troubles come and my heart burdened be;
Then I am still and wait here in the silence,
Until you come and sit awhile with me.

You raise me up, so I can stand on mountains;
You raise me up to walk on stormy seas;
I am strong when I am on your shoulders;
You raise me up to more than I can be.

There is no life - no life without its hunger;
Each restless heart beats so imperfectly;
But when you come and I am filled with wonder,
Sometimes, I think I glimpse eternity.

You raise me up, so I can stand on mountains;
You raise me up to walk on stormy seas;
I am strong when I am on your shoulders;
You raise me up to more than I can be.

Josh Groban

JANUARY

MONDAY 9

Ideas control the world

TUESDAY 10

Laughter is more contagious than tears

Open the door to your heart. If you open the door any one can go in and out. On the other hand, if the door is too narrow, everyone will bump into it. Life is happiest when you are needed by others and can do things for others. A loving heart is the most beautiful thing in the world.

Cheng Yen

WEDNESDAY 11

Spend time with friends

THURSDAY 12

Be kind to everyone, including yourself

FRIDAY 13

Get up early to get a head start

SATURDAY 14

A family is a strong support network

SUNDAY 15

Face the reality of the world with courage

JANUARY

MONDAY **16**

Do the things you don't like doing first

TUESDAY **17**

There is no one in the world just like you

FRIENDSHIP

**A true friend knows your weakness,
but shows you your strengths;
Feels your fears, but fortifies your faith;
Sees your anxieties, but frees your spirit;
Recognises your disabilities, but
emphasises your possibilities.**

William Arthur Ward

WEDNESDAY **18**

You are more capable than you know

happy

At all times and under all circumstances, we have the power to transform the quality of our lives.

Werner Erhard

THURSDAY 19

Necessity is the mother of invention

FRIDAY 20

If it's worth doing, it's worth doing well

SATURDAY 21

Bad money habits are serious

SUNDAY 22

Tears are words the heart can't explain

JANUARY

THE DILEMMA

To laugh is to risk appearing a fool.
To weep is to risk appearing sentimental.
To reach out for another is to risk involvement.
To expose feelings is to risk rejection.
To place your dreams before a crowd is to risk ridicule.
To love is to risk not being loved in return.
To go forward in the face of overwhelming odds is to risk failure.
But risks must be taken, because the greatest hazard in life is
to risk nothing.
The person who risks nothing, does nothing, has nothing, is nothing.
He may avoid suffering and sorrows but he cannot learn, feel,
change, grow or love.
Chained by his certitudes, he is a slave – he has forfeited his freedom.
Only a person who takes risks is truly free.

MONDAY **23**

We become like the people we associate with

TUESDAY **24**

Be master of your habits, or they will master you

Don't ruin an apology with an excuse.

WEDNESDAY 25

Don't complicate your life

THURSDAY 26

Technology is just a tool – use it wisely

FRIDAY 27

There are no stupid questions

SATURDAY 28

Think before you act

SUNDAY 29

Promises are made to be kept

MONDAY **30**

When you say "thank you", mean it

TUESDAY **31**

Keep your heart free from hate

True happiness is to enjoy the present, without anxious dependence upon the future, not to amuse ourselves with either hopes or fears but to rest satisfied with what we have, which is sufficient, for he that is so wants nothing. The greatest blessings of mankind are within us and within our reach. A wise man is content with his lot, whatever it may be, without wishing for what he has not.

Lucius Annaeus Seneca

Is minic cuma aingeal ar an diabhal féin.

There is often the look of an angel on the devil himself.

Ní mar a shíltear a bhítear.

Things are not always as they seem.

spriocanna

GOALS

FEABHRA
FEBRUARY

> In the long run, we shape our lives, and we shape ourselves. The process never ends until we die. And the choices we make are ultimately our own responsibility.
>
> *Eleanor Roosevelt*

WEDNESDAY 1

See the good in others

THURSDAY 2

Only you have your special talents

All your dreams can come true if you have the courage to pursue them.

Walt Disney

I wanted a perfect ending. Now I've learned, the hard way, that some poems don't rhyme, and some stories don't have a clear beginning, middle, and end. Life is about not knowing, having to change, taking the moment and making the best of it, without knowing what's going to happen next. Delicious Ambiguity.

Gilda Radner

FEBRUARY

But I, being poor, have only my dreams;
I have spread my dreams under your feet;
Tread softly because you tread on my dreams.

WB Yeats

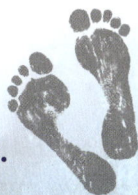

If you can DREAM IT, you can DO IT.

Whatever you can do, or dream you can, begin it. Boldness has genius, power and magic in it.

Goethe

FRIDAY 3

Take the inititive

SATURDAY 4

Choose your friends carefully

SUNDAY 5

Care about those who care about you

FEBRUARY

Keep YOUR ENERGY UP

To do anything in this world worth doing, we must not stand back shivering and thinking of the cold and danger, but jump in and scramble through as best we can.

Sidney Smith

Don't be too timid and squeamish about your actions. All life is an experiment.

Ralph Waldo Emerson

What if our religion was each other
If our practice was our life
If prayer, our words.
What if the temple was the earth,
If forests were our church,
If holy water – the rivers, lakes, and oceans.
What if meditation was our relationships,
If the teacher was life,
If wisdom was self-knowledge,
If love was the centre of our being.

Ganga White

When we least expect it, life sets us a challenge to test our courage and willingness to change; at such a moment, there is no point in pretending that nothing has happened or in saying that we are not yet ready. The challenge will not wait. Life does not look back. A week is more than enough time for us to decide whether or not to accept our destiny.

Paulo Coelho

MONDAY 6

Be generous and fair to everyone

TUESDAY 7

Respect your body

WEDNESDAY 8

Let yourself be inspired by a great purpose

The harder the battle, the sweeter the victory.

Les Brown

FEBRUARY

THURSDAY 9

Feel good about your achievements

FRIDAY 10

Use your intuition

SATURDAY 11

Get enough sleep

Trust thyself; every heart vibrates to that inner string.

Ralph Waldo Emerson

SUNDAY 12

Take courage and ask for what you need

Until you make peace with who you are
you will never be content with what you have.

Doris Mortman

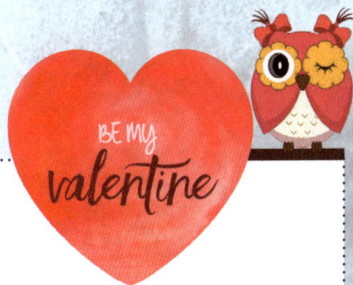

MONDAY 13

Conquer a bad habit

TUESDAY 14
St Valentine's Day

Be generous with your love

WEDNESDAY 15

Be on the lookout for new opportunities

THURSDAY 16

Do today what you want to put off until tomorrow

**Dwell on the beauty of life.
Watch the stars, and see
yourself running with them.**

Marcus Aurelius

FEBRUARY

*Choose to be kind rather than to be right and
you'll be right every time.*

FRIDAY 17

Don't be afraid of criticism

SATURDAY 18

Stop and daydream; let your imagination roam free

SUNDAY 19

Start as you mean to go on

Be at least as interested in
what goes on inside you as
what happens outside. If
you get the inside right the
outside will fall into place.

Eckhart Tolle

Life is a series of natural and spontaneous changes. Don't resist them; that only creates sorrow. Let reality be reality. Let things flow naturally forward in whatever way they like.

Lao Tzu

MONDAY 20

To win you must first begin

TUESDAY 21

Develop a habit of optimism

WEDNESDAY 22

Pursue your goals

THURSDAY 23

Think big

If you don't stand for something, you'll fall for anything.

Happiness is not trying or finding; it's deciding.

Osiris

FRIDAY 24

Get excited about life

SATURDAY 25

Stand back to see the bigger picture

SUNDAY 26

Patience is a virtue

Love begins with a smile, grows with a kiss, and ends with a teardrop.

FEBRUARY

*Believe in yourself, for you are
marvellously endowed.
Believe in your job, for all honest
work is sacred.
Believe in this day, for every minute
contains an opportunity to do good.
Believe in your family, and create
harmony by trust and cooperation.
Believe in your neighbour, for the more
friends you can make, the happier you will be.
Believe in uprightness, for you cannot go wrong doing right.
Believe in your decisions; consult God first, then go ahead.
Believe in your health; your health is your wealth. Don't doubt it.
Believe in the now; yesterday is past recall, and tomorrow
may never come.
Believe in God's promises; He means it when He says.
"I am with you always."
Believe in God's mercy; if God forgives you,
you can forgive yourself and try again tomorrow.*

MONDAY **27**

Enjoy what you do, and do what you enjoy

TUESDAY **28**

In the game of life, be a good sport

spriocanna
GOALS

MÁRTA
MARCH

Mol an óige agus tiocfaidh sí.
Praise the youth and they will flourish.

Is minic a bhíonn ciúin ciontach.
The quiet one is often guilty.

Tending your garden is not just about growing flowers. It's about taking time for things that matter to you, including nurturing yourself.

ABC of loving families

Accept each member as the unique gift they are.
Balance work, rest and play.
Communicate with mutual respect.
Demonstrate how love encourages growth.
Embrace the changes the years bring.
Find ways to say 'I love you'.
Generate self esteem and self acceptance.
Help each other do for themselves.
Inspire independence and interdependence.
Juggle schedules to 'be there'.
Know there are no perfect families.
Look for the best in each other.
Make the world a better place.
Nurture abilities and talents.
Openly talk about whatever is up.
Provide safety and security.
Quickly mend fences and move on.
Remind each other of their greatness.
Savour memories and traditions.
Take time to really listen and care.
Understand how precious family time is.
Value presence more than presents.
Work things out compassionately.
Xperience life's ups and downs together.
Yearn to create a happy home.
Zeal to bequeath a legacy of love.

@meiji stewart

WEDNESDAY 1

Join in and participate fully

MARCH

Souls love. That's what souls do. Egos don't, but souls do. Become a soul, look around, and you'll be amazed – all the beings around you are souls. Be one, see one.

Ram Dass

I heard what you said. I'm not the silly romantic you think. I don't want the heavens or the shooting stars. I don't want gemstones or gold. I have those things already. I want – a steady hand. A kind soul. I want to fall asleep, and wake, knowing my heart is safe. I want to love, and be loved.

Shana Abe

THURSDAY **2**

Listen to others as you would like others to listen to you

FRIDAY **3**

Everyone's opinion is valid

SATURDAY **4**

Self expression is essential for happiness

Drop your fears and
pick up your dreams.
The world needs dreamers
like you. You are the light
of a brighter world.

Liam Tinker

*People are always blaming
their circumstances for what they are.
I don't believe in circumstances. The people
who get on in this world are the people who get
up and look for the circumstances they want,
and if they can't find them, make them.*

George Bernard Shaw

Keep your thoughts positive, because
your thoughts become your words.
Keep your words positive, because
your words become your behaviors.
Keep your behaviors positive, because
your behaviors become your habits.
Keep your habits positive, because
your habits become your values.
Keep your values positive, because
your values become your destiny.

Ghandi

SUNDAY **5**

Speak clearly so people can understand you

You're never too old to play.

MONDAY **6**

A helping hand is worth more than good advice

> *Be soft. Do not let the world make you hard. Do not let the pain make you hate. Do not let the bitterness steal your sweetness.*
>
> Kurt Vonnegut

TUESDAY **7**

One who looks for a friend without faults, will find none

WEDNESDAY **8**

In a moment of doubt, believe in yourself

THURSDAY **9**

Learn more about healthy nutrition

MARCH

> You're gorgeous, you old hag, and if I could give you just one gift ever for the rest of your life it would be this – confidence. It would be the gift of confidence. Either that or a scented candle.
>
> *David Nicholls*

FRIDAY 10

Money often costs too much

SATURDAY 11

Practise your skills and become more skilled

SUNDAY 12

Be careful what you wish for

MARCH

Angry people want you to see how powerful they are.
Loving people want you to see how powerful you are.

Chief Red Eagle

MONDAY **13**

No one can be grateful and unhappy at the same time

There is a time for everything and a season for every activity under heaven: a time to be born and a time to die, a time to plant and a time to uproot, a time to kill and a time to heal, a time to tear down and a time to build, a time to weep and a time to laugh, a time to mourn and a time to dance, a time to scatter stones and a time to gather them, a time to embrace and a time to refrain, a time to search and a time to give up, a time to keep and a time to throw away, a time to tear and a time to mend, a time to be silent and a time to speak, a time to love and a time to hate, a time for war and a time for peace.

Ecclesiastes 3:1-8

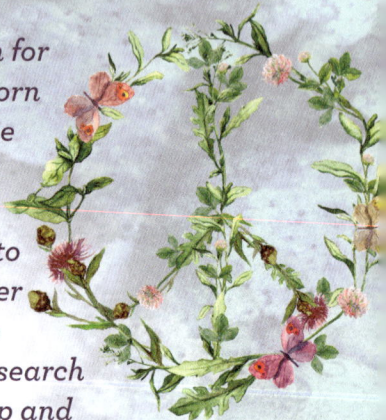

TUESDAY **14**

When you forgive others, you also are forgiven

Live without pretending.
Love without depending.
Listen without defending.
Speak without offending.

WEDNESDAY 15

Accept your work with a cheerful heart

THURSDAY 16

It is always a good time to learn something new

FRIDAY 17
Happy ☘ St. Patricks Day

Your creativity is always in demand

Challenges are what make life interesting and overcoming them is what makes life meaningful.

MARCH

*Don't wait for the perfect moment;
take the moment and make it perfect.*

SATURDAY 18

Don't make assumptions

SUNDAY 19

Your contribution is unique and valuable

The past is a place of reference, not a place of residence.

For me music is a vehicle to bring our pain to the surface, getting it back to that humble and tender spot where, with luck, it can lose its anger and become compassion again.

Paula Cole

YOUR ANTI-STRESS KIT

RUBBER BAND
To remind you to stretch your ideas and your mind to new limits so you will continue to grow and reach your potential.

TISSUE
To remind you to see the tears and needs of others, including those of yourself and your peers.

CANDY KISS
To remind you that everyone needs a hug, a kiss, or a word or two of encouragement every day.

LIFE SAVER
To remind you to think of your peers as your "life savers", to care about each other and help each other through the stressful times that occur in life.

PENNY
To remind you the value of your thoughts – BIG ones and little ones! Share them with others. It's what you do with them that counts'

ERASER
To remind you that we all make mistakes and with an eraser they can be erased, even human mistakes can be corrected and leave no trace..

TOOTHPICK
To remind you to 'pick out' the small irritating items that get in the way of appreciating the good qualities in ourselves and others, and to be tolerant and accepting of differences.

PAPER CLIP
It's important to "keep it all together." Find the balance in your physical, professional, and spiritual life. Explore the resources and programs available to your community.

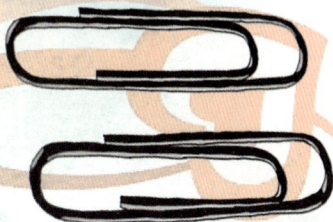

MARCH

Out of clutter, find simplicity.
Albert Einstein

MONDAY **20**

Your health is precious, take good care of it

TUESDAY **21**

Be your own best friend

WEDNESDAY **22**

Tomorrow is another day

THURSDAY **23**

Don't overdramatise your life

FRIDAY **24**

Finish what you start

A mother is the truest friend we have, when trials heavy and sudden fall upon us; when adversity takes the place of prosperity; when friends desert us; when trouble thickens around us, still will she cling to us, and endeavor by her kind precepts and counsels to dissipate the clouds of darkness, and cause peace to return to our hearts.

Washington Irving

The formative period for building character for eternity is in the nursery. The mother is queen of that realm, and sways a sceptre more potent than that of kings or priests.

SATURDAY 25

Most of what you worry about, never happens

SUNDAY 26
Mother's Day

Little things can make a big difference

Impossible only means you haven't found the solution yet.

MONDAY **27**

We are all worthy of love

TUESDAY **28**

Trust that everything will work out perfectly

WEDNESDAY **29**

Give to life exactly what you want to get from life

THURSDAY **30**

The difference between 'a champ' and 'a chump' is U

FRIDAY **31**

The one thing you can give, and still keep, is your word

spriocanna

GOALS

AIBREÁN
APRIL

Is fearr an tsláinte ná na táinte.
Health is better than wealth.

It's never too late to start over. If you wern't happy with yesterday, try something different today, and risk it being better tomorrow. Don't stay stuck, make your own luck.

SATURDAY 1

Don't take yourself so seriously

SUNDAY 2

The person wrapped up in themselves is a very small package

APRIL

MONDAY 3

Give more, expect less

TUESDAY 4

Triumph is just 'umph' added to 'try'!

WEDNESDAY 5

It's never right to do wrong, and it's never wrong to do right

THURSDAY 6

Make a list of things you like about yourself

FRIDAY 7

Never allow one dispute to injure a friendship

IMPORTANT WORDS FROM STEVE JOBS

I reached the pinnacle of success in the business world. In others' eyes, my life is an epitome of success. However, aside from work, I have little joy. In the end, wealth is only a fact of life that I am accustomed to. At this moment, lying on the sick bed and recalling my whole life, I realise that all the recognition and wealth that I took so much pride in, have paled and become meaningless in the face of impending death. In the darkness, I look at the green lights from the life supporting machines and hear the humming mechanical sounds, I can feel the breath of god of death drawing closer... Now I know we should pursue other matters that are unrelated to wealth...

Should be something that is more important: perhaps relationships, perhaps art, perhaps a dream from younger days ... Non-stop pursuing of wealth will only turn a person into a twisted being, just like me. God gave us the senses to let us feel the love in everyone's heart, not the illusions brought about by wealth. The wealth I have won in my life I cannot bring with me. What I can bring is only the memories precipitated by love. That's the true riches which will follow you, accompany you, giving you strength and light to go on. Love can travel a thousand miles. Life has no limit. Go where you want to go. Reach the height you want to reach. It is all in your heart and in your hands. What is the most expensive bed in the world? "Sick bed" ... You can employ someone to drive the car for you, make money for you but you cannot have someone to bear the sickness for you. Material things lost can be found. But there is one thing that can never be found when it is lost – "Life". When a person goes into the operating room, he will realise that there is one book that he has yet to finish reading – "Book of Healthy Life". Whichever stage in life we are at right now, with time, we will face the day when the curtain comes down. Treasure love for your family, love for your spouse, love for your friends... Treat yourself well. Cherish others.

APRIL

The will to win, the desire to succeed, the urge to reach your full potential... these are the keys that will unlock the door to personal excellence.

Having the confidence to be yourself in a world which is doing its best to make you doubt yourself, is the greatest gift you can give yourself and the greatest act of rebellion you can ever perform.

Death leaves a heartache no one can heal, love leaves a memory no one can steal.

From an Irish headstone

SATURDAY **8**

Seek first to understand, then to be understood

SUNDAY **9**

Mind your moods, they can wreak havoc

*It's a funny thing about life;
if you refuse to accept anything
but the best, you very often get it.*

W Somerset Maugham

**Choose a job you
love, and you will
never have to work
a day in your life.**
Confuscius

MONDAY **10**

Design a weekly exercise schedule

TUESDAY **11**

Encourage others

WEDNESDAY **12**

Failure is temporary, giving up makes it permanent

THURSDAY **13**

Don't expect others to be like you

APRIL

May your choices reflect your hopes, not your fears.

Nelson Mandela

FRIDAY 14
Good Friday

Those who gossip to you, will gossip about you

SATURDAY 15

Learn to communicate responsibly

SUNDAY 16
Easter Sunday

Laughter is good medicine

I have seen too many dear friends leave this world too soon; before they understood the great freedom that comes with aging.

It's not our job to toughen our children to face a cruel and heartless world. It's our job to raise children who will make the world a little less cruel and heartless.

LR Knost

I would never trade my amazing friends, my wonderful life or my loving family for less grey hair or a flatter belly.

MONDAY 17
Bank holiday

Be aware that all your actions have consequences

TUESDAY 18

Spend some time listening to your favourite music

WEDNESDAY 19

Put a little extra effort in today

THURSDAY 20

Don't rush to judgement

Sure, over the years my heart has been broken. How can your heart not break when you lose a loved one, or when a child suffers, or even when somebody's beloved pet gets hit by a car? But broken hearts are what give us strength and understanding and compassion. A heart never broken is pristine and sterile and will never know the joy of being imperfect.

Whose business is it if I choose to read or play on the computer until 4am and sleep until noon?

FRIDAY 21

Be happy for no reason

SATURDAY 22

There is no fun in negative thinking

SUNDAY 23

Decide what you want and go for it

APRIL

Fall in love with as many things as possible.

I am not going to live forever, but while I am still here, I will not waste time lamenting what could have been, or worrying about what will be. And I shall eat dessert every single day (if I feel like it).

MONDAY 24

Be kind, it shows

TUESDAY 25

Trust is the foundation of any relationship

WEDNESDAY 26

You are as strong and powerful as you allow yourself to be

So, to answer your question,
I like being old. It has set me free.
I like the person I have become.

WILD
FREE

THURSDAY 27

Words are powerful tools, and can be dangerous

FRIDAY 28

Speak up, there are no mind readers

SATURDAY 29

It's ok to change your mind, just let people know

SUNDAY 30

Keep true to yourself

I am so blessed to have lived long enough to have my hair turning grey, and to have my youthful laughs be forever etched into deep grooves on my face. So many have never laughed, and so many have died before their hair could turn silver.

Trí ní is deacair a thuiscint:
intleacht na mban,
obair na mbeach,
teacht agus imeacht na taoide.

Three things hardest to understand:
womens' intuition,
the work of the bees,
the coming and going of the tide.

spriocanna
GOALS
BEALTAINE
MAY

MAY

The only thing we have to fear is fear itself.

Franklin D Roosevelt

MONDAY **1**
Bank holiday

Exercise your brain, exercise your body – fire up your life

TUESDAY **2**

A friend's eye is a good mirror

WEDNESDAY **3**

Indulge in good eating habits

THURSDAY **4**

Nothing is as far away as one minute ago

"It's impossible," said pride;
"It's risky," said experience;
"It's pointless," said reason;
"Give it a try," whispered the heart.

*If we wait until we are ready,
we will be waiting for the
rest of our lives.*

FRIDAY **5**

Action produces results, nothing else

SATURDAY **6**

Self image and self esteem come from your inner 'self'

SUNDAY **7**

Add enthusiasm to every venture

*The practice of
forgiveness is our
most important
contribution to the
healing of the world.*

Marianne Williamson

CHILDREN LEARN WHAT THEY LIVE

If children live with criticism they learn to condemn.

If children live with hostility they learn to fight

If children live with fear, they learn to be apprehensive

If children live with pity, they learn to feel sorry for themselves.

If children live with ridicule, they learn to be shy.

If children live with jealousy, they learn to feel envy.

If children live with tolerance, they learn to be patient

If children live with shame, they learn to feel guilty

If children live with encouragement, they learn to be confident.

If children live with praise, they learn to appreciate.

If children live with approval, they learn to like themselves

If children live with acceptance, they learn to find love in the world.

If children live with recognition, they learn it is good to have a goal.

If children live with sharing, they learn to be generous.

If children live with honesty and fairness, they learn about truth and justice.

If children live with kindness and consideration, they learn respect.

If children live with security, they learn to have faith in themselves and those around them.

If children live with friendliness, they learn that the world is a nice place in which to live.

If children live with serenity, they will have peace of mind.

With what are our children living?

Adapted from Dorothy L Nolte

MONDAY **8**

Plan your work and work your plan

MAY

Keep a notebook –
if only for the sake
of making space in
your own head.

TUESDAY 9

Be a proud role model for young people

WEDNESDAY 10

Honesty is ALWAYS the best policy

THURSDAY 11

Don't look for a shortcut through, just look for the best way round

FRIDAY 12

Pay attention to what is going on around you

MAY

The most important kind of freedom is the freedom to express who we truly are without fear that we will not be good enough for others.

SATURDAY 13

There is nothing about you that is wrong

SUNDAY 14

You will always see what you are looking for

THINGS MY MOTHER TAUGHT ME

My mother taught me to appreciate a job well done: "If you are going to kill each other – do it outside. I've just finished cleaning." My mother taught me religion: "You better pray that will come out of the carpet". My mother taught me about time travel: "If you don't straighten up, I'm going to knock you into the middle of next week". My mother taught me reason: "Because I said so, that's why!" My mother taught me logic: "If you fall out of that swing and break your neck, you're not going shopping with me". My mother taught me foresight: "Make sure you wear clean underwear, in case you're in an accident". My mother taught me irony: "Keep crying and I'll give you something to cry about". My mother taught me about science of osmosis: "Shut your mouth and eat your breakfast". My mother taught me about contortionism: "Will you look at the dirt on the back of your neck?" My mother taught me about stamina: "You'll sit there until all that dinner is finished".

Somewhere over the rainbow
Way up high,
There's a land that I heard of
Once in a lullaby.
Somewhere over the rainbow
Skies are blue,
And the dreams that you dare to dream
Really do come true.
Someday I'll wish upon a star
And wake up where the clouds are far behind me,
Where troubles melt like lemon drops
Way above the chimney pots,
That's where you'll find me.
Somewhere over the rainbow
Bluebirds fly.
If birds fly over the rainbow
Why then, oh why can't I?
If happy little bluebirds fly
beyond the rainbow,
Why, oh why, can't I?

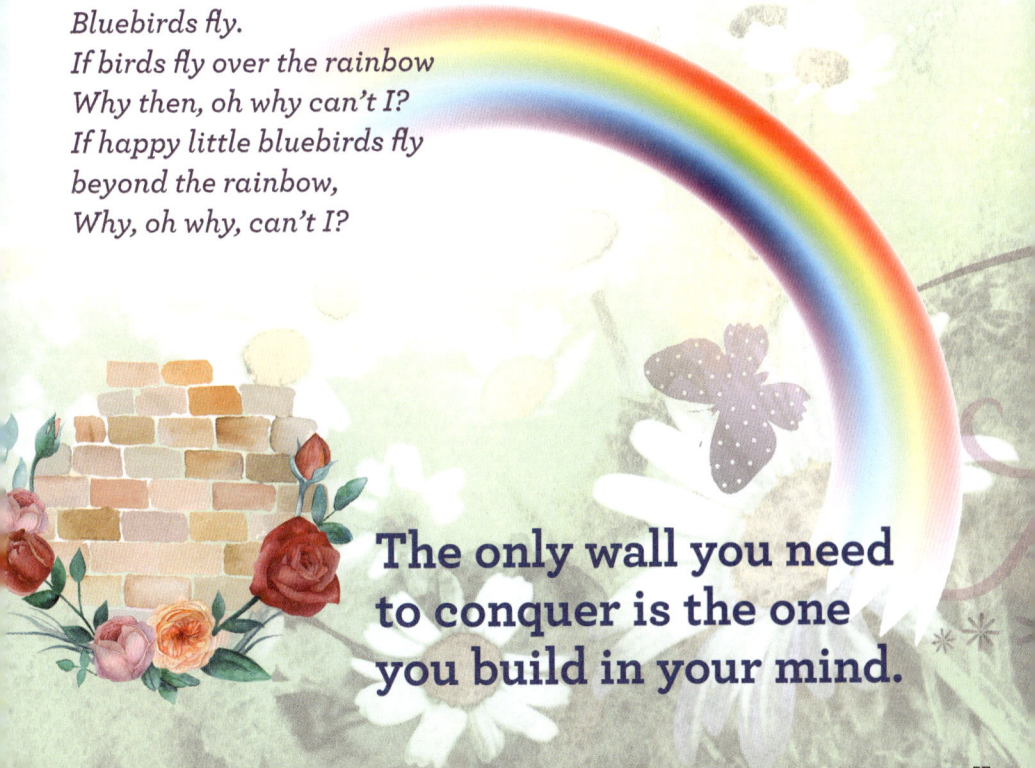

**The only wall you need
to conquer is the one
you build in your mind.**

MAY

It is not what you do for your children, but what you have taught them to do for themselves, that will make them successful human beings.

Ann Landers

MONDAY **15**

Don't believe everything you hear

TUESDAY **16**

Be a master of your actions, not a master of re-actions

WEDNESDAY **17**

Your time will come, have patience

THURSDAY **18**

Don't look back in anger or regret

Give people more than they expect and do it cheerfully. Never laugh at anyone's dreams; people who don't have dreams, don't have much. Great love and great achievements involve great risk. Remember the three Rs – Respect for self, Respect for others, Responsibility for all your actions. Smile when picking up the phone; the caller can hear it in your voice. When you lose, don't lose the lesson. When you say "I love you", mean it. Marry someone you like to talk to. When you get older, their conversational skills will be as important as any other.

FRIDAY 19

Accept people as you find them

SATURDAY 20

Be someone who makes a difference for another

SUNDAY 21

Compassion and kindness work wonders

The worst sin toward our fellow creatures is not to hate them, but to be indifferent to them: that's the essence of inhumanity.

George Bernard Shaw

MAY

Most people would rather be certain they're miserable than risk being happy.

Robert Anthony

Our best successes often come after our greatest disappointments.

Henry Ward Beecher

Our deeds determine us as much as we determine our deeds.

George Eliot

MONDAY **22**

It's never boring when you're playing to win

TUESDAY **23**

Those who follow the crowd are quickly lost in it

WEDNESDAY **24**

Attitudes are caught, not taught

Remember happiness starts with you; not with your relationship, nor your friends, nor your job, but with you. You bring your happiness with you to your relationships, your friends and your job.

THURSDAY **25**

Don't compare yourself with others

FRIDAY **26**

Share your ideas

SATURDAY **27**

Stop judging yourself, and you will stop judging others

SUNDAY **28**

Generate courage and self-confidence

One of the secrets of a long and fruitful life is to forgive everybody everything every night before you go to bed.

MONDAY 29

Your thoughts determine how you feel

TUESDAY 30

Learn from someone you admire

WEDNESDAY 31

Thank a friend for being your friend

Always be yourself. Never try to hide who you are. Stand up for what you believe in. Never regret the past. There was a reason for everything. Every mistake, every 'terrible thing' that happened to you, every moment of weakness, has served its purpose. You have survived. You have grown. You have learned. Acknowledge how far you have come. Never apologise for the battles you have won. The only shame is to have a shame you're ashamed of. Be proud of who you have become.

If you haven't found it yet, keep looking.

Steve Jobs

spriocanna
GOALS
MEITHEAMH
JUNE

_____
_____
_____
_____
_____
_____
_____
_____

**Aithníonn ciaróg
ciaróg eile.**
*It takes one to
know one.*

*He who can give thanks
for little will always
find he has enough.*

**Ní neart go
cur le chéile.**
*Unity is
strength.*

**Sometimes you have to die a little inside
in order to be reborn and rise again as a
stronger and wiser version of you.**

JUNE

The grass is greener where you water it.

THURSDAY 1

Find an activity that you love to do, and do it

FRIDAY 2

Develop good leadership skills

Your task is not to seek for love, but merely to seek and find all the barriers within yourself that you have built against it.

Rumi

Don't wish your days away, waiting for better ones ahead. Enjoy the day you're spending now.

It takes a big heart to help shape little minds.

IF

If you can keep your head when all about you
   Are losing theirs and blaming it on you,
If you can trust yourself when all men doubt you,
   But make allowance for their doubting too;
If you can wait and not be tired by waiting,
   Or being lied about, don't deal in lies,
Or being hated, don't give way to hating,
   And yet don't look too good, nor talk too wise:
If you can dream—and not make dreams your master;
   If you can think—and not make thoughts your aim;
If you can meet with Triumph and Disaster
   And treat those two impostors just the same;
If you can bear to hear the truth you've spoken
   Twisted by knaves to make a trap for fools,
Or watch the things you gave your life to, broken,
   And stoop and build 'em up with worn-out tools:
If you can make one heap of all your winnings
   And risk it on one turn of pitch-and-toss,
And lose, and start again at your beginnings
   And never breathe a word about your loss;
If you can force your heart and nerve and sinew
   To serve your turn long after they are gone,
And so hold on when there is nothing in you
   Except the Will which says to them: 'Hold on!'
If you can talk with crowds and keep your virtue,
   Or walk with Kings—nor lose the common touch,
If neither foes nor loving friends can hurt you,
   If all men count with you, but none too much;
If you can fill the unforgiving minute
   With sixty seconds' worth of distance run,
Yours is the Earth and everything that's in it,
   And—which is more—you'll be a Man, my son!

Rudyard Kipling

JUNE

Be strong enough to let go.

SATURDAY 3

With life as your teacher, you will never stop learning

SUNDAY 4

Be responsible for all your own actions, and inactions

YOUR GREATEST POWER IS THE POWER TO BE

To be loving.
To be courageous.
To be joyful.
To be friendly.
To be kind.
To be aware.
To be forgiving.
To be tolerant.
To be patient.
To be humble.
To be helpful.
To be there.
To be a great human being.
To be here.

Worrying is like praying for what you don't want.

Holding on to anger is like grasping a hot coal with the intent of throwing it at someone else. You are the one who gets burned.

MONDAY 5
Bank holiday

Have a good time

TUESDAY 6

Allow yourself to be 'infected' by enthusiasm

WEDNESDAY 7

Time heals almost everything. Give time, time

THURSDAY 8

Look at the world with a broad, generous and friendly eye

JUNE

To do good you actually have to do something.

FRIDAY 9

Competition is healthy, cooperation is priceless

SATURDAY 10

Be where you are, there is no where else

SUNDAY 11

Value yourself, you are worthy of love and respect

The I in illness is isolation, and the crucial letters in wellness are WE.

WE

There is no such thing as a bad day, just bad moments that we insist on carrying all day long!

We are now at a point in time when the ability to receive, store, transform and transmit data — the lowest cognitive form — has expanded literally beyond comprehension. Understanding and wisdom are largely forgotten as we struggle under an avalanche of information.

Dee Hock

We are supposed to enjoy the good stuff now, while we can, with the people we love. Life has a funny way of teaching us that lesson over and over again.

Family isn't always blood. It's the people in your life who want you in theirs; the ones who accept who you are; the ones who want to see you smile and the ones who love you — no matter what.

A father is someone who carries pictures where his money used to be.

Lion

JUNE

If you're going through hell, keep going.

Winston Churchill

MONDAY 12

Say 'please' and 'thank you', it is always appreciated

TUESDAY 13

Tackle a problem bigger than yourself

WEDNESDAY 14

Make a small improvement in some area

THURSDAY 15

When in doubt, just do what you know to be right

FRIDAY 16

Forgive an old friend

You have been criticising yourself for years
and it hasn't worked. Try approving of yourself
and see what happens.

Louise L Hay

SATURDAY 17

The best of life's possibilities are right here, right now

SUNDAY 18
Father's Day

Refuse to be sidetracked by your own excuses

Don't waste your time trying to 'get even'. It doesn't work.
What you give out always comes back to you. So drop the
past and work on loving yourself in the now. Raise your
self-esteem to such a level that you only allow loving
experiences in your life. Then you will have a
wonderful future.

Louise Hay

Now and again, it's
good to pause in the
pursuit of happiness
and just be happy.

*Any time we witness an injustice and do not act,
we train our character to be passive in its presence,
and therby eventually lose all ability to defend
ourselves and those we love.*

Julian Assange

Stress: The inability to tell the difference between what you think is happening and what is actually happening.

MONDAY **19**

Every choice you make is a turn your life takes

TUESDAY **20**

All blame is a waste of time

WEDNESDAY **21**

Don't get bogged down in self-pity

THURSDAY **22**

Be motivated to help others by empathy and compassion

If you would only understand the power of your smile, you would never stop smiling.

JUNE

Sleep and rest fixes many things

FRIDAY 23

Sing and dance to your own music

SATURDAY 24

Learn the rules and play the game of life to win

SUNDAY 25

Let go of any heavy baggage that is weighing you down

AT 6: Mummy I love you.
At 10: Mum, you're so annoying.
At 16: WHATEVER!
At 18: I'm leaving!
AT 25: Mum you were right.
At 35: Will we go shopping?
At 50: I don't want to lose my mum.
At 70: I would give anything for my mum to be here with me.

MONDAY 26

Let life happen, but make things happen in life

TUESDAY 27

See the world through grateful eyes

WEDNESDAY 28

Appreciate the love of your family

THURSDAY 29

Be patient. Be kind. Everyone has their own struggles

FRIDAY 30

Don't take anything personally, unless it's a compliment

Knowledge comes from books.
Wisdom comes from life.

spriocanna
GOALS

IÚIL
JULY

_____
_____
_____
_____
_____
_____
_____
_____
_____
_____
_____
_____

When you flip the switch in that attic,
it doesn't matter whether it's been dark for
ten minutes, ten years or ten decades.

**An té a bhíonn siúlach,
bíonn sé scéalach,
agus an té a bhíonn scéalach
bíonn sé bréagach.**

_The man who travels tells stories, and
the man who tells stories tells lies._

JULY

Darkness cannot drive out darkness: only light can do that. Hate cannot drive out hate: only love can do that.

Martin Luther King Jr

It's never too late to take a moment to look.

Sharon Salzberg

It is never too late to turn on the light. Your ability to break an unhealthy habit or turn off an old tape doesn't depend on how long it has been running; a shift in perspective doesn't depend on how long you've held on to the old view.

SATURDAY 1

We can learn something from everything

SUNDAY 2

It is the way it is, deal with it

The light illuminates the room and banishes the murkiness, letting you see the things you couldn't see before.

Doubt is a virus that attacks our self-esteem, productivity and confidence. Faith, that you and your life are unfolding perfectly, is the strongest vaccine.

Sean Stephenson

JUST LAUGH

Make the most of today.
Get interested in something.
Shake yourself awake.
Let the winds of enthusiasm
sweep through you.
Live today with GUSTO.

Dale Carnegie

Look deep into nature,
and then you will understand
everything better.

Albert Einstein

IN THIS HOUSE:
We make mistakes.
We say "I'm sorry".
We give second chances.
We have fun.
We share.
We give hugs.
We cherish friends.
We forgive.
We are patient.
We laugh out loud.
We don't take each other for granted.
We love.
We are home.

NOTE TO SELF:
Relax.
You are enough.
You do enough.
You have enough.

JULY

MONDAY 3

The work will only get done in the doing of it

TUESDAY 4

Keep inventing new goals

WEDNESDAY 5

Don't take anything or anyone for granted

THURSDAY 6

Be at peace with who you are

FRIDAY 7

Never give up on your dreams

WISHES AND BLESSINGS

May today there be peace within.
May you trust your highest power
that you are exactly where you are meant to be.
May you not forget the infinite possibilities that
are born of faith.
May you use those gifts that you have received,
and pass on the love that has been given to you.
May you be content knowing you are a child of God.
Let this presence settle into your bones,
and allow your soul the freedom
to sing, dance, and to bask in the sun.
It is there for each and every one of you.

SATURDAY 8

There is nothing to fear in the future

SUNDAY 9

Everything can change in the blink of an eye

JULY

Take criticism seriously, but not personally. If there is truth or merit in the criticism, try to learn from it. Otherwise, let it roll right off you.

Hillary Clinton

MONDAY 10

Better late than never

TUESDAY 11

Listen to what others are saying

WEDNESDAY 12

Everything can be resolved in a conversation

What we call the beginning is often the end. And to make an end is to make a beginning. The end is where we start from.

TS Eliot

The soul that sees beauty may sometimes walk alone.

Johann Wolfgang von Goethe

Become genuinely interested in other people. Be a good listener. Encourage others to talk about themselves.

Dale Carnegie

THURSDAY 13

Know that you are never alone

FRIDAY 14

Good personality is fine, but good character is above all else

SATURDAY 15

Be trustworthy, so people know they can rely on you

SUNDAY 16

Acknowledge your parents, they gave you life

JULY

Some women choose to follow men, and some women choose to follow their dreams. If you're wondering which way to go, remember that your career will never wake up and tell you that it doesn't love you anymore.

Lady Gaga

MONDAY 17

Want it more than anything? Excelerate your efforts

TUESDAY 18

Don't be limited by limited thinking

WEDNESDAY 19

Explore and learn about your world

THURSDAY 20

Life is a voyage of discovery

We realise the importance of our voices only when we are silenced.

Yousafzai

Just don't give up trying to do what you really want to do. Where there is love and inspiration, I don't think you can go wrong.

Ella Fitzgerald

inspire someone today

FRIDAY 21

There are not many certainties in life, I'm certain about that

SATURDAY 22

Everyone deserves to be heard, so LISTEN

SUNDAY 23

Keep your minds eye firmly on what you want to achieve

The girls who were unanimously considered beautiful often rested on their beauty alone. I felt I had to do things, to be intelligent and develop a personality in order to be seen as attractive. By the time I realised maybe I wasn't plain and might even possibly be pretty, I had already trained myself to be a little more interesting and informed.

Diane Von Furstenberg

JULY

MONDAY 24

All is well, keep going, keep growing

Each second we live is a new and unique moment of the universe, a moment that will never be again. And what do we teach our children? We teach them that two and two make four, and that Paris is the capital of France. When will we also teach them what they are? We should say to each of them: Do you know what you are? You are a marvel. You are unique. In all the years that have passed, there has never been another child like you. Your legs, your arms, your clever fingers, the way you move. You may become a Shakespeare, a Michelangelo, a Beethoven. You have the capacity for anything. Yes, you are a marvel. And when you grow up, can you then harm another who is, like you, a marvel? You must work, we must all work, to make the world worthy of its children.

Pablo Picasso

TUESDAY 25

Every day is a new chance to start again

> *I am only one, but still I am one. I cannot do everything, but still I can do something; and because I cannot do everything, I will not refuse to do something that I can do.*
>
> *Helen Keller*

WEDNESDAY **26**

Learn to enjoy your own company

THURSDAY **27**

Forgive a friend for a perceived hurt

FRIDAY **28**

Love yourself just the way you are

SATURDAY **29**

Sometimes criticism is constructive

SUNDAY **30**

Peace begins in your own heart

MONDAY **31**

Look for opportunities to help others

spriocanna
GOALS
LÚNASA
AUGUST

you must create

Is minic ubh mhór ag cearc bheag.
A small hen often has a large egg.

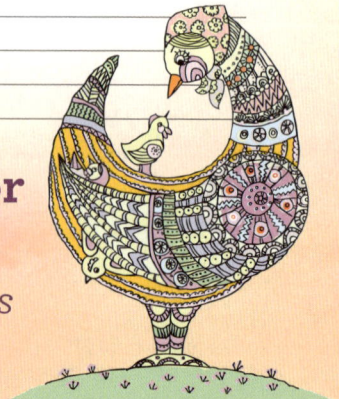

> Ideas are worthless, until
> you get them out of your head
> and put them to work.

10 secrets for success and inner peace

Have a mind that is open to everything and attached to nothing.

Don't die with your music still inside you.

You can't give away what you don't have.

Embrace silence.

Give up your personal drama.

You can't solve a problem with the same mind that created it.

There are no justified resentments.

Treat yourself as if you already are where you'd like to be.

Treasure your divinity.

Wisdom is avoiding all thoughts that weaken you.

Dr Wayne Dyer

TUESDAY 1

Write things down

WEDNESDAY 2

He who flings mud, generally loses ground

AUGUST

LOVE

love you

It is the greatest, most powerful force in the universe.
It's a treasure that people would give anything for,
yet it costs nothing to give or receive.
There is an endless supply, and it can be shared
with family, friends and strangers.
It increases positivity, and acts like a soul shield
against negativity from the outside world.
It forgives, trusts, encourages, inspires, and makes
all who have it into better people.
It is the the truth, the path, and the way.
Love: Give it, Receive it, and Believe in it.

Doe Zantamata

The women whom I love and admire for their strength and
grace did not get that way because s*** worked out. They got that
way because s*** went wrong and they handled it. They handled
it in a thousand different ways on a thousand different days,
but they handled it. These women are my superheroes.

Elizabeth Gilbert

*It is easy to love the people far away. It is not
always easy to love those close to us. It is easier to
give a cup of rice to relieve hunger than to relieve
the loneliness and pain of someone unloved in
our own home. Bring love into your home for
this is where our love for each other must start.*

Mother Teresa

I want to grow old without facelifts...
I want to have the courage to be loyal
to the face I've made. Sometimes I
think it would be easier to avoid old
age, to die young, but then you'd
never complete your life, would you?
You'd never wholly know you.

Marilyn Monroe

THURSDAY 3

Your words are powerful, don't spread an untruth

FRIDAY 4

All change involves loss

SATURDAY 5

When you lose, don't lose the lesson

SUNDAY 6

Life has lots of turning points

AUGUST

I know why familles were created, with all their imperfections. They humanise you. They are made to make you forget yourself occasionally, so that the beautiful balance of life is not destroyed.

Anaïs Nin

MONDAY 7
Bank holiday

Listen to a new kind of music

TUESDAY 8

The world is your oyster

WEDNESDAY 9

Don't suffer in silence

THURSDAY 10

Tackle your problems head on

Hurt people hurt people. That's how pain patterns get passed on, generation after generation. Break the suffering – punishment cycle today. Forgive and forget about finding fault. Meet fear with courage, anger with empathy, contempt with compassion, cruelty with kindness. Greet grimaces with smiles. Hate is the weapon that perpetuates the wrongs of the past. Love is the tool that builds a new and desirable future.

LIFE IS ART

I think everything in life is Art, what you do, how you dress, that way you love someone, how you talk, your smile and your personality, what you believe in and all your dreams, the way you drink your tea and how you decorate your home or party, your grocery list, the food you make, how your writing looks and the way you feel.

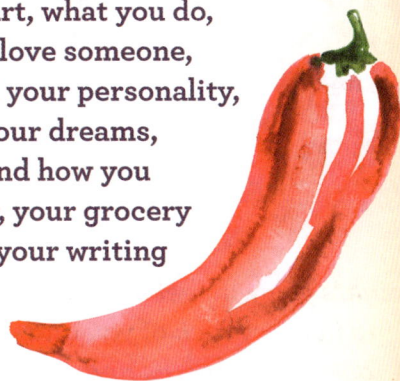

People are like stained-glass windows. They sparkle and shine when the sun is out, but when the darkness sets in, their true beauty is revealed only if there is light from within.

Elisabeth Kubler-Ross

AUGUST

My mission, should I choose to accept it, is to find peace with exactly who and what I am. To take pride in my thoughts, my appearance, my talents, my flaws and to stop this incessant worrying that I can't be loved as I am.

Anaïs Nin

Some nights you will feel like there are a thousand galaxies exploding in every inch of you and you are burning too bright to ever be looked at directly, and some nights you will feel impossibly small, like your whole body could slip through the spaces between atoms and never reappear in this world again, and some nights you will feel like a paper doll, carefully crafted and easily blown away, fragile, too delicate to ever be touched, and some nights you will feel like each cell in your body is made of the strength that holds the whole planet together, and that is okay because you are made of stardust and miniscule atoms and breakable bones and the building blocks of everything in the universe, and you are too alive to never feel anything more than human.

Alicia

The thing that is really hard, and really amazing, is giving up on being perfect and beginning the work of becoming yourself.

Anna Quindlen

FRIDAY 11

Everything will result from your choice

SATURDAY 12

What we give, we get

Life is too short to wake up in the morning with regrets. So, love the people who treat you right, forget about the ones who don't and believe everything happens for a reason. If you get a chance, take it. If it changes your life, let it. Nobody said it would be easy, they just promised it would be worth it.

SUNDAY 13

Worry causes wrinkles

AUGUST

You gain strength, courage and confidence
by every experience in which you really stop to
look fear in the face. You are able to say to yourself,
"I lived through this horror. I can take the next
thing that comes along." You must do
the thing you think you cannot do.

Eleanor Roosevelt

MONDAY 14

Think the best of everything

TUESDAY 15

Forget past mistakes and concentrate on future success

WEDNESDAY 16

Always do your best

THURSDAY 17

Wherever you are, be there

I am not afraid. I was born to do this.

Joan of Arc

FRIDAY 18

Expect the unexpected

SATURDAY 19

Where there are true friends there is true wealth

I believe in pink. I believe laughing is the best calorie burner. I believe in kissing, kissing a lot. I believe in being strong when everything seems to be going wrong. I believe that happiest girls are the prettiest. I believe that tomorrow is another day and I believe in miracles.

Audrey Hepburn

SUNDAY 20

Life is an adventure – be adventurous

I love to see a young girl go out and grab the world by the lapels. Life's a bitch. You've got to go out and kick ass.

Maya Angelou

MONDAY **21**

Goals are dreams with deadlines

TUESDAY **22**

All glory comes from daring to begin

WEDNESDAY **23**

Dreams are the stuff of progress

THURSDAY **24**

The best sight is insight

Though I am grateful for the blessings of wealth, it hasn't changed who I am. My feet are still on the ground. I'm just wearing better shoes.

Oprah Winfrey

AUGUST

How different our lives are when we really know what is deeply important to us, and keeping that picture in mind, we manage ourselves each day to be and to do what really matters most.

Stephen R Covey

FRIDAY 25

Be committed to excellence

SATURDAY 26

Fortune favours the brave

SUNDAY 27

Anger is one letter short of danger

If you obey all the rules, you miss all the fun.

Katharine Hepburn

MONDAY 28

Only complain to someone who can do something about it

TUESDAY 29

Things don't always turn out as we would like

WEDNESDAY 30

Try and fail, but don't fail to try

I've come to believe that each of us has a personal calling that's as unique as a fingerprint – and that the best way to succeed is to discover what you love and then find a way to offer it to others in the form of service, working hard, and also allowing the energy of the universe to lead you.

Oprah Winfrey

THURSDAY 31

Be good, do good

Is fearr Gaeilge bhriste ná Bearla cliste.

Broken Irish is better than clever English.

spriocanna

GOALS

MEÁN FOMHAIR
SEPTEMBER

Keep your words soft and sweet, you may have to eat them later

SEPTEMBER

I am Me. In all the world, there is no one else exactly like me. Everything that comes out of me is authentically mine, because I alone chose it – I own everything about me: my body, my feelings, my mouth, my voice, all my actions, whether they be to others or myself.

I own my fantasies, my dreams, my hopes, my fears. I own my triumphs and successes, all my failures and mistakes. Because I own all of me, I can become intimately acquainted with me. By so doing, I can love me and be friendly with all my parts.

I know there are aspects about myself that puzzle me, and other aspects that I do not know – but as long as I am friendly and loving to myself, I can courageously and hopefully look for solutions to the puzzles and ways to find out more about me. However I look and sound, whatever I say and do, and whatever I think and feel at a given moment in time is authentically me. If later some parts of how I looked, sounded, thought, and felt turn out to be unfitting, I can discard that which is unfitting, keep the rest, and invent something new for that which I discarded. I can see, hear, feel, think, say, and do.

I have the tools to survive, to be close to others, to be productive, and to make sense and order out of the world of people and things outside of me. I own me, and therefore, I can engineer me. I am me, and I am okay.

Virginia Satir

listen to the sea

May the sun bring you new energy by day.
May the moon softly restore you by night.
May the rain wash away your worries.
May the breeze blow new strength into your being
May you walk gently on the earth and know its beauty all the days of your life.

SATURDAY 2

Respect yourself and respect others

SUNDAY 3

You are everything to somebody

Education commences at the mother's knee, and every word spoken within the hearing of little children tends towards the formation of character. Let parents bear this forever in mind.

Hosea Ballou

SEPTEMBER

Even the darkest night will end and the sun will rise.

Victor Hugo

MONDAY 4

Think good and kind thoughts to feel better

TUESDAY 5

Have a beautiful day

WEDNESDAY 6

Education is your best friend for life

THURSDAY 7

Be the hero of your own story

The most common way people give up their power is by thinking they don't have any.

Alice Walker

Our deepest fear is not that we are inadequate. Our deepest fear is that we are powerful beyond measure. It is our light, not our darkness that most frightens us. We ask ourselves, 'Who am I to be brilliant, gorgeous, talented, fabulous?' Actually, who are you not to be? You are a child of God. Your playing small does not serve the world. There is nothing enlightened about shrinking so that other people won't feel insecure around you. We are all meant to shine, as children do. We were born to make manifest the glory of God that is within us. It's not just in some of us; it's in everyone. And as we let our own light shine, we unconsciously give other people permission to do the same. As we are liberated from our own fear, our presence automatically liberates others.

Marianne Williamson

FRIDAY **8**

Be the best you that you can be

SATURDAY **9**

Your life only gets better when you get better

SUNDAY **10**

Everyone is the artist of their own life

SEPTEMBER

MONDAY 11

Experience is what you get when you don't get what you want

TUESDAY 12

The best way out is always through

WEDNESDAY 13

Whether you think you can, or think you can't, you're right

THURSDAY 14

Give up, give in or give it all you've got

FRIDAY 15

Achieve and maintain a healthy weight

hope

Hope believes in life when it seems like no one else does.
Hope opens doors where despair closes them.
Hope lights a candle instead of cursing the darkness.
Hope discovers something can be done instead of
resigning itself to "nothing".
Hope draws its power from deep trust in a divine
God and the basic goodness in humankind.
Hope seeks out the good in situations
instead of assuming the worst.
Hope regards problems, small or large,
as opportunities for growth.
Hope loves life and the chance to dance with it.
Hope does not yield to fear or cynicism.
Hope sets big goals and is not frustrated
by difficulties or setbacks.
Hope pushes ahead when it would be easy to quit.
Hope puts up with modest gains, realising that
the longest journey starts with the first step.
Hope is a good companion as it brings the divine
assurance of final victory.

SATURDAY **16**

Always be on time

SUNDAY **17**

Take responsibility for the choices you make every day

Life lives, life dies. Life laughs, life cries.
Life gives up and again life tries.
Life looks different through everyone's eyes.

MONDAY **18**

Choose friends who are truthful and open

TUESDAY **19**

Have the courage to admit when you're wrong

The creation of a more peaceful and happier society has to begin from the level of the individual, and from there, it can expand to one's family, one's neighbourhood, one's community – one's society, one's country, one's world.

Compassion for others begins with kindness to ourselves.

Simplicity is the ultimate sophistication.
Leonardo DaVinci

WEDNESDAY **20**

Focus on your positive qualities

SEPTEMBER

> I belive there is an inner power
> that makes winners or losers.
> And the winners are the ones
> who really listen to the truth
> of their hearts.
>
> *Sylvester Stallone*

THURSDAY **21**

Laugh and the world laughs with you

FRIDAY **22**

Don't doubt your capacity to cope

SATURDAY **23**

Show consideration for others

SUNDAY **24**

Be aware that your actions have consequences

SEPTEMBER

Nothing in the world can take the place of persistence. Talent will not; nothing is more common than unsuccessful men with talent. Genius will not; unrewarded genius is almost a proverb. Education will not: the world is full of educated derelicts. Persistence and determination alone are omnipotent. The slogan 'press on' has solved and will always solve the problems of the human race.

Calvin Coolidge

You cannot connect the dots looking forwards; you can only connect them looking backwards. So you have to trust that the dots will somehow connect in your future. You have to trust in something – your gut, destiny, life, karma, whatever. This approach has never let me down, and it has made all the difference in my life.

Steve Jobs

MONDAY 25

It's you who says who you are

> **Sunshine is delicious, rain is refreshing, wind braces us up, snow is exhilarating; there is really no such thing as bad weather, only different kinds of good weather.**
>
> *John Rushkin*

TUESDAY 26

Give more than is expected of you

WEDNESDAY 27

All your future lies ahead

THURSDAY 28

Winners are generous

FRIDAY 29

Be grateful

SATURDAY 30

Life isn't fair, but it is still good

Never discourage anyone who continually makes progress, no matter how slow.
Plato

spriocanna

GOALS

DEIREADH
FOMHAIR

OCTOBER

Is glas iad na cnoic i bhfad uainn.
The faraway hills are green.

SUNDAY **1**

The best way to break a habit is to drop it

Do not wait for leaders.
Do it alone, person to person.
Mother Teresa

MONDAY 2

Every expert was once a beginner

To make the right choices in life, you
have to get in touch with your soul. To do this
you need to experience solitude, which most
people are afraid of, because in the silence you
hear the truth and know the solutions.
Deepak Chopra

TUESDAY 3

The only person you can be is yourself

WEDNESDAY 4

However good or bad a situation is, it will change

THURSDAY 5

Get up, dress up and show up

OCTOBER

BE

Be your own best friend.
Be your own teacher.
Be the guiding light in your life.
Be your own source of wisdom.
Be a person you love and respect.
Be your own inspiration.
Be your own motivation.
Be the greatest joy in your life.
Be true to yourself and honour who you are.
Every day of your life.

FRIDAY 6

No one is in charge of your happiness but you

SATURDAY 7

Choose your friends and let your friends choose you

SUNDAY 8

Don't hurt anyone intentionally, even yourself

Motivation is what gets you started. Habit is what keeps you going.

MONDAY **9**

Design your own future

If you are not willing to risk the unusual, you will have to settle for the ordinary.

Jim Rohn

TUESDAY **10**

Acceptance is a sure key to happiness

WEDNESDAY **11**

Everything matters

THURSDAY **12**

Treasure every moment you have on this earth

OCTOBER

Don't wait for time. *Make it.*
Don't wait for love. *Feel it.*
Don't wait for money. *Earn it.*
Don't wait for a path to appear. *Look for it.*
Don't wait for opportunity. *Find it.*
Don't settle for less. *Go for the best.*
Don't compare. *Be unique.*
Don't fight your misfortune. *Transform it.*
Don't avoid failure. *Learn from it.*
Don't dwell on a mistake. *Get over it.*
Don't go back. *Go forward.*
Don't close your mind. *Open your heart.*
Don't run from life. *Embrace it.*

FRIDAY 13

Develop an enthusiastic attitude

SATURDAY 14

Allow yourself to experience the joy of winning

SUNDAY 15

Explore the world of the creative arts

MONDAY **16**

Challenge your own limits

Don't let someone who gave up on their dreams talk you out of going after yours.

TUESDAY **17**

Don't believe everything you think

WEDNESDAY **18**

Talk it over with someone you trust

THURSDAY **19**

Criticism is just another person's opinion

FRIDAY **20**

Let yourself be inspired

OCTOBER

The most important kind of freedom is the freedom to express who we truly are without fear that we will not be good enough for others.

Storms make trees take deeper roots.

Nothing ever happened in the past, it happened in the now. Nothing will ever happen in the future, it will happen in the NOW.

Eckhart Tolle

SATURDAY **21**

Be strong. Be brave. Be true

SUNDAY **22**

Grant others the freedom to be themselves

The amount of happiness you have in your life depends on the amount of freedom you have in your heart.

Thich Nhat Hanh.

> ## Never separate the life you live from the words you speak.
> *Paul Wellstone*

MONDAY 23

A great life is no accident

TUESDAY 24

Value your life; keep yourself safe

WEDNESDAY 25

Be patient; it is the way of nature

THURSDAY 26

Don't weigh yourself down with worries and doubts

FRIDAY 27

Hold on to your dreams

OCTOBER

WHO AM I?

I am your constant companion.
I am your greatest helper or heaviest burden.
I will push you on to success or drag you down to failure.
I am completely at your command.
Half the things you do, you might as well turn over to me and
I will be able to do them quickly and correctly.
I am easily changed, I learn quickly, you must merely be firm with me.
Show me exactly what you want done and, after a few attempts,
I will get it done for you.
I am the servant of all great men and alas of all failures as well.
Those who are great, I have made great.
Those who are failures I have made failures.
I am not a machine though I work with all the precision of a machine.
You may run me for profit or use me for ruin, it makes
no difference to me.
Take me, train me, be firm with me, and I will put the world at your feet.
Be lazy with me, and I will destroy you
Who am I?
I am ATTITUDE.

SATURDAY **28**

It's normal to make mistakes, that's how we learn

SUNDAY **29**

When stopped, just take the next small step

MONDAY 30
Bank holiday

Go for a walk and take in the view

TUESDAY 31

Tell special people how special they are

I am thankful for:
The mess I have to clean up after a party –
it means I have friends.
The taxes I have to pay – it means that I have a job.
The clothes that fit me tightly – it means I have
enough food to eat.
A lawn that needs cutting, windows that need
cleaning, guttering that needs fixing – it means
that I have a home.
The parking space I find on the far side of the
parking lot – it means that I can walk.
My huge electricity bill – it means that I am clean
and warm.
The piles of laundry and ironing – it means that
I have clothes to wear.
I am thankful for the complaining I hear about our
government – it means that I have freedom of speech.
I appreciate the fact that I can read this message –
it means that I can read.
I am thankful for weariness and aching muscles at the
end of the day – it means that I have been productive.
And the alarm that goes off in the morning –
IT MEANS THAT I AM ALIVE!

HALLOWEEN

119

**Má bhíonn tú ag lorg cara gan locht,
beidh tú gan chara go deo.**

*If you are looking for a friend without a fault,
you will be without a friend forever.*

spriocanna
GOALS
SAMHAIN
NOVEMBER

**Maireann croí
éadrom i bhfad.**

*A light heart
lives longest.*

**Beware of the half truth, you may
have gotten hold of the wrong half.**

Music gives a soul to the universe, wings to the mind, flight to the imagination and life to everything.

Plato

To be creative means to be in love with life. You can be creative only if you love life enough that you want to enhance its beauty. You want to bring a little more music to it, a little more poetry to it, a little more dance to it.

Osho

WEDNESDAY 1

Balance diet and exercise for good health

THURSDAY 2

The best things in life are not things

NOVEMBER

"IT MUST BE EASY FOR HER"

The next time this thought creeps into your mind, remember this: It isn't easy for any of us. To overcome the past, to forget the pain we have suffered, to let go, to get up when we are tired, to smile when we feel like crying. Yet, there are gifts in all experiences and we can make a choice to see the light even in dark places.

FRIDAY 3

Always put your best foot forward

SATURDAY 4

Never fear to tell the truth

SUNDAY 5

Life would be dull without human error

Your worst enemy cannot harm you as much as your own unguarded thoughts.
Buddha

The most important decision you make is to be in a good mood.
Voltaire

MONDAY 6

Don't be a problem for others

TUESDAY 7

When the going gets tough, keep going

WEDNESDAY 8

Take time to think about what you want

THURSDAY 9

Don't create your own upsets

NOVEMBER

We can complain because rose bushes have thorns, or rejoice because thorn bushes have roses.

FRIDAY 10

Accept that nobody is perfect

SATURDAY 11

Keep your heart free from hate

SUNDAY 12

It is by rising to the challenge that we learn how to be brave

A smile is a woman's best accessory; sequins are appropriate no matter what the occasion; and some days simply require a glass of champagne.

The world is full of magic things waiting for our senses to grow sharper.

WB Yeats

MONDAY 13

Practice forgiveness

TUESDAY 14

Get rid of the 'BUT' in your life

WEDNESDAY 15

If you don't know how to do something... ask!

THURSDAY 16

Attitude is everything

We do not inherit the earth from our ancestors, we borrow it from our children.

An awful lot of things had to go terribly wrong for me to end up in the right place.

NOVEMBER

Everything you are against, weakens you;
Everything you are for, empowers you.

Wayne Dyer

Opportunity is missed by most people because it is dressed in overalls and looks like work.

The power of 1

One song can spark a moment
One flower can wake the dream
One tree can start a forest
One bird can herald spring
One smile begins a friendship
One handclasp lifts a soul
One star can guide a ship at sea
One word can frame the goal
One vote can change a nation
One sunbeam lights a room
One candle wipes out darkness
One laugh will conquer gloom
One step must start each journey
One word must start each prayer
One hope will raise our spirits
One touch can show you care
One voice can speak with wisdom
One heart can know what's true
One life can make the difference
You see, it's up to you!!

Author Unknown

Remember that children, marriages and flower gardens reflect the kind of care they get.

H Jackson Browne

FRIDAY 17

Anything is possible

Be yourself.
Accept yourself.
Value yourself.
Forgive yourself.
Bless yourself.
Express yourself.
Trust yourself.
Love yourself.
Empower yourself.

A flower does not think of competing with the flower next to it, it just blooms.

SATURDAY 18

Read about people you admire

SUNDAY 19

Dream more while you are awake

NOVEMBER

MONDAY **20**

Maturity is accepting imperfection

TUESDAY **21**

Greed will eventually burn even the lucky

WEDNESDAY **22**

The smarter you work the more luck you will have

Is suffering really necessary? Yes and no.
If you had not suffered as you had, there would be
no depth to you as a human being, no humility, no
compassion. You would not be reading this now.
Suffering cracks open the shell of ego, and then comes
a point when it has served its purpose. Suffering is
necessary until you realise it is unnecessary.

Eckhart Tolle

The best way to appreciate something is to be without it for a while.

THURSDAY 23

Accepting responsibility is the key to personal freedom

FRIDAY 24

'Someday' is far away

SATURDAY 25

Your community has everything you need

SUNDAY 26

You can be an inspiration to others

Remember your happiness starts with you, not with your relationship, your friends or your job, but with YOU.

NOVEMBER

Your best teacher is your last mistake.

Ralph Nader

MONDAY 27

Never speak badly about yourself

TUESDAY 28

You are in charge of the thoughts you think

WEDNESDAY 29

Don't indulge in confusion

THURSDAY 30

The most wasted of all days is the one without laughter

CHRISTMAS SHOPPING LIST

1. Buy a 2018 Get Up and Go Diary for all my friends.

2. Buy a Get Up and Go Travel Journal and plan my next trip.

SPRIOCANNA
GOALS

Slán abhaile.
Safe home.

Don't wish your days away, waiting for better ones ahead. Enjoy the day you are spending now.

Dá fhada an lá tagann an tráthnóna.
However long the day, evening will come.

I scath a chéile a mhaireann na daoine.
We all exist in each others' shadows.

FRIDAY 1

Change the way you think about a problem

SATURDAY 2

Make promises and keep them

Happiness comes when we stop complaining about the troubles we have and offer thanks for all the troubles we don't have.

May God bless you and keep you.
May God's face shine upon you and be gracious unto you.
May God give you the grace not to sell yourself short,
Grace to risk something big for something good,
Grace to remember that the world is now too dangerous
for anything but truth, and too small for anything but love.
May God take your eyes and see through them.
May God take your lips and speak through them.
May God take your hands and work through them.
May God take your heart, and set it on fire.

SUNDAY 3

Make it happen

DECEMBER

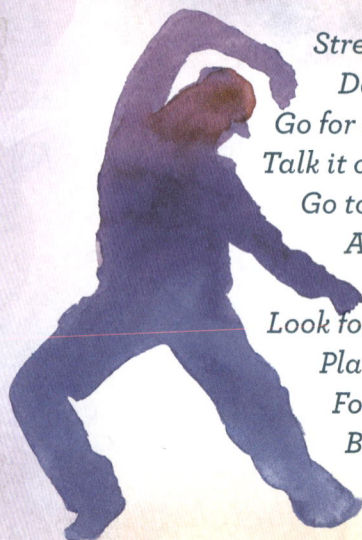

Stress less.
Dance it out.
Go for a walk.
Talk it over.
Go to bed early.
Ask for a hug.
Be grateful for what you have.
Look for solutions.
Plan a day out with friends.
Focus on what you can do.
Be the victor, not the victim.

Always laugh when you can. It's cheap medicine.

Lord Byron

MONDAY 4

Decide who you want to be and be that

TUESDAY 5

Think kindly of everyone; everyone is struggling with something

---

WEDNESDAY 6

If you want the fruit, you must climb the tree

It often takes more courage to change one's opinion than to keep it.

Willy Brandt

THURSDAY **7**

Don't let your world spin out of control

FRIDAY **8**

Enjoy shopping for gifts

SATURDAY **9**

Get plenty of fresh air and exercise

SUNDAY **10**

Be curious, not judgemental

Life's treasures are people – together.

Patricia Ann Goodman

You do not climb a mountain so that the world can see you. You climb a mountain so that you can see the world.

I PROMISE MYSELF

To be so strong that nothing can disturb my peace of mind. **To talk health**, happiness and prosperity to every person I meet. **To make all my friends feel** that there is something worthwhile in them. **To look at the sunny side** of everything and make my optimism come true. **To think only of the best**, to work only for the best and to expect only the best. **To be just as enthusiastic** about the success of others as I am about my own. **To forget the mistakes** of the past and press on to the greater achievements of the future. **To wear a cheerful expression** at all times and give a smile to every living creature I meet. **To give so much time** to improving myself that I have no time to criticise others. **To be too large for worry**, too noble for anger, too strong for fear and too happy to permit the presence of trouble. **To think well of myself** and to proclaim this fact to the world, not in loud words, but in great deeds. **To live in faith** that the whole world is on my side, so long as I am true to the best that there is in me.

Christian D Larson

MONDAY **11**

We are all ordinary, and we can all be extraordinary

136

DECEMBER

TUESDAY 12

Spend time reading a good book

You cannot hope to build a better world without improving the individuals. To that end, each of us must work for his or her own improvement, and at the same time, share a general responsibility for all of humanity, our particular duty being to aid those to whom we think we can be most useful.

Marie Curie

WEDNESDAY 13

Be interested in the world around you

THURSDAY 14

Don't hide the love that lives within you

DECEMBER

As I've aged, I've become kinder to myself, and less critical of myself. I've become my own friend. I don't chide myself for eating that extra cookie, or for not making my bed, or for buying that silly cement gecko that I didn't need, but looks so 'avante garde' on my patio. I am entitled to a treat, to be messy, to be extravagant.

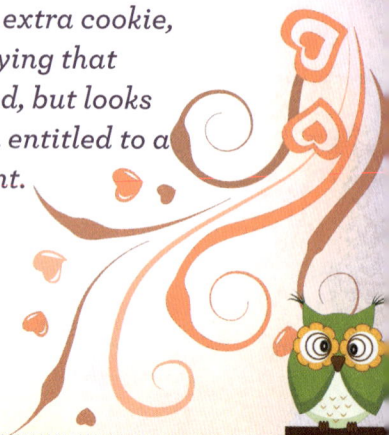

FRIDAY 15

Self expression is essential to life

SATURDAY 16

To earn more you must learn more

SUNDAY 17

Everything you need is inside yourself

**Being someone's first LOVE
may be great,
but to be their last
is beyond PERFECT.**

20 THINGS TO START DOING

Go to bed earlier.
Focus on my future.
Drink a lot of water and green tea.
Eat fruit, vegetables and natural foods.
Go for a walk, swim or a bike ride every week.
Read a new book or 10 every month.
Enjoy and be grateful for the little things.
Avoid processed food.
Begin yoga or meditation.
Make a to do list and start doing.
Stretch daily to increase my flexibility.
Listen to peaceful music.
Keep my living space tidy.
Wear clothes that make me look good.
Give away or sell things I don't need.
Eat a big breakfast, average lunch and tiny dinner.
Know that the efforts I make now will repay me later.
Only think positive thoughts about people and things.
Spend more time outdoors.
Keep a diary or journal.

**Whatever happened over the past
year, be thankful for where it has
brought you. You are exactly where
you are meant to be.**

DECEMBER

MONDAY 18

Grant yourself permission to choose

I will walk the beach in a swim suit that is stretched over a bulging body, and will dive into the waves with abandon if I choose to, despite the pitying glances from the jet set.

Unknown

TUESDAY 19

Always stay in the 'here and now', and regularly plan for 'then'

WEDNESDAY 20

In each of us there's a little of all of us

THURSDAY 21

Be specific about who, what, where, when, and why

The man who does not read has no advantage over the man who cannot read.

Oscar Wilde

FRIDAY 22

Learn to manage your money

Healing your own heart is the single most powerful thing you can do to change the world. Your own transformation will enable you to withdraw so completely from evil that you contribute to it by not one word, one thought, or one breath. This healing process is like recovering your soul from fear and suffering.

Deepak Chopra

SATURDAY 23

Care for those who care

SUNDAY 24

Be prepared to be surprised

DECEMBER

Celebrate the love of friends and family

WITH EVERY WISH
FOR A VERY
MERRY
CHRISTMAS
AND
THE HAPPIEST
New Years

A CHRISTMAS BLESSING

During this Christmas season,
may you be blessed
with the spirit of the season
which is peace;
the gladness of the season
which is hope;
and the heart of the season
which is love.

It's not what's under the tree that matters; it's who is gathered around it.

When you become calm and serene on the inside, the world becomes more calm and serene on the outside.

*As I unclutter my life,
I free myself to answer
the callings of my soul.*

TUESDAY **26**

Take time to relax and be grateful for all you have

WEDNESDAY **27**

Acknowledge yourself for your achievements

THURSDAY **28**

Make a vision board of your current desires

FRIDAY 29

Be open to the possibility of miracles

SATURDAY 30

Smooth seas never made skilful sailors

SUNDAY 31

Every end is a new beginning

Cheers to a new year and another chance for us to get it right.

Oprah Winfrey

Infuse your life with action. Don't wait for it to happen. Make it happen. Make your own future. Make your own hope. Make your own love. And whatever your beliefs, honour your creator, not by passively waiting for grace to come down from upon high, but by doing what you can to make grace happen... yourself, right now, right down here on Earth.

Bradley Whitford

DESIDERATA

Go placidly amid the noise and haste, and remember what peace there may be in silence. As far as possible without surrender be on good terms with all persons. Speak your truth quietly and clearly, and listen to others, even the dull and ignorant; they too have their story.

Avoid loud and aggressive persons, they are vexations to the spirit. If you compare yourself with others, you may become vain and bitter; for always there will be greater and lesser persons than yourself. Enjoy your achievements as well as your plans. Keep interested in your own career, however humble; it is a real possession in the changing fortunes of time. Exercise caution in your business affairs; for the world is full of trickery. But let this not blind you to what virtue there is; many persons strive for high ideals; and everywhere life is full of heroism.

Be yourself. Especially, do not feign affection. Neither be cynical about love; for in the face of all aridity and disenchantment it is perennial as the grass. Take kindly the counsel of the years, gracefully surrendering the things of youth. Nurture strength of spirit to shield you in sudden misfortune. But do not distress yourself with imaginings. Many fears are born of fatigue and loneliness. Beyond a wholesome discipline, be gentle with yourself.

You are a child of the universe, no less than the trees and the stars; you have a right to be here. And whether or not it is clear to you, no doubt the universe is unfolding as it should. Therefore be at peace with God, whatever you conceive Him to be; and whatever your labours and aspirations, in the noisy confusion of life keep peace with your soul. With all its sham, drudgery and broken dreams, it is still a beautiful world. Be cheerful. Strive to be happy.

Max Ehrmann

2018 CALENDAR

JANUARY

Mon	Tue	Wed	Thu	Fri	Sat	Sun
1	2	3	4	5	6	7
8	9	10	11	12	13	14
15	16	17	18	19	20	21
22	23	24	25	26	27	28
29	30	31				

FEBRUARY

Mon	Tue	Wed	Thu	Fri	Sat	Sun
			1	2	3	4
5	6	7	8	9	10	11
12	13	14	15	16	17	18
19	20	21	22	23	24	25
26	27	28				

MARCH

Mon	Tue	Wed	Thu	Fri	Sat	Sun
			1	2	3	4
5	6	7	8	9	10	11
12	13	14	15	16	17	18
19	20	21	22	23	24	25
26	27	28	29	30	31	

APRIL

Mon	Tue	Wed	Thu	Fri	Sat	Sun
						1
2	3	4	5	6	7	8
9	10	11	12	13	14	15
16	17	18	19	20	21	22
23	24	25	26	27	28	29
30						

MAY

Mon	Tue	Wed	Thu	Fri	Sat	Sun
	1	2	3	4	5	6
7	8	9	10	11	12	13
14	15	16	17	18	19	20
21	22	23	24	25	26	27
28	29	30	31			

JUNE

Mon	Tue	Wed	Thu	Fri	Sat	Sun
				1	2	3
4	5	6	7	8	9	10
11	12	13	14	15	16	17
18	19	20	21	22	23	24
25	26	27	28	29	30	

JULY

Mon	Tue	Wed	Thu	Fri	Sat	Sun
						1
2	3	4	5	6	7	8
9	10	11	12	13	14	15
16	17	18	19	20	21	22
23	24	25	26	27	28	29
30	31					

AUGUST

Mon	Tue	Wed	Thu	Fri	Sat	Sun
		1	2	3	4	5
6	7	8	9	10	11	12
13	14	15	16	17	18	19
20	21	22	23	24	25	26
27	28	29	30	31		

SEPTEMBER

Mon	Tue	Wed	Thu	Fri	Sat	Sun
					1	2
3	4	5	6	7	8	9
10	11	12	13	14	15	16
17	18	19	20	21	22	23
24	25	26	27	28	29	30

OCTOBER

Mon	Tue	Wed	Thu	Fri	Sat	Sun
1	2	3	4	5	6	7
8	9	10	11	12	13	14
15	16	17	18	19	20	21
22	23	24	25	26	27	28
29	30	31				

NOVEMBER

Mon	Tue	Wed	Thu	Fri	Sat	Sun
			1	2	3	4
5	6	7	8	9	10	11
12	13	14	15	16	17	18
19	20	21	22	23	24	25
26	27	28	29	30		

DECEMBER

Mon	Tue	Wed	Thu	Fri	Sat	Sun
					1	2
3	4	5	6	7	8	9
10	11	12	13	14	15	16
17	18	19	20	21	22	23
24	25	26	27	28	29	30
31						

NOTES

Visit our **website** to find your nearest stockist.
Check out our website or Facebook page for
new products coming soon.

The Irish Get Up And Go Diary €10/£7.50
The Irish Get Up And Go Diary Special Edition €15/£12.50
The Get Up and Go Diary for Girls €10/£7.50
The Get Up and Go Diary for Boys €10/£7.50
The Get Up and Go Diary €10/£7.50
The Get Up and Go Diary for Busy Women €10/£7.50
The Get Up and Go Travel Journal €12/£10
Homework Journal for Students €14/£11

GetUpandGo

DON'T MISS OUT ON NEXT YEARS DIARY. ORDER NOW FOR 2018!

Follow us on Facebook
www.facebook.com/TheIrishGetUpAndGoDiary

Follow us on Twitter
twitter @getupandgo1

Available directly by order form here:

(P+P €2.50/£2.00 PER COPY)
PLEASE PRINT YOUR NAME AND ADDRESS CLEARLY

Send me _____ Copies of _____

Name: _____

Address: _____

_____

_____

I enclose cheque/postal order for _____

Contact number/ email _____

Send your order to:
Get Up and Go Publications Ltd
Cambo Line
Hazelwood
Sligo
F91 NP04
Ireland.

Tel: 00353 71 914 6717
00353 86 178 8631

Purchase of 8+ items
P+P €1 per item